VELOCIRAPTOR

A TRUE BOOK

by
Elaine Landau

Children's Press®
A Division of Grolier Publishing

New York London Hong Kong Sydney
Danbury, Connecticut

An artist's impression of *Velociraptor*

Reading Consultant
Linda Cornwell
*Coordinator Of School Quality
And Professional Improvement
Indiana State Teachers Association*

Science Consultant
James O. Farlow
*Indiana University-
Purdue University Fort Wayne
Department of Geosciences*

Dedication:
For Brenna Joy Tudor

Visit Children's Press® on the Internet at:
http://publishing.grolier.com

Library of Congress Cataloging-in-Publication Data

Landau, Elaine.
    Velociraptor / by Elaine Landau.
        p.   cm. — (A true book)
    Includes bibliographical references and index.
    Summary: Describes the characteristics and habits of the small
but fierce meat-eating dinosaur that lived in prehistoric times.
    ISBN 0-516-20437-8 (lib. bdg.)   0-516-26509-1 (pbk.)
    1. Velociraptor—Juvenile literature.   [1. Velociraptor.
2. Dinosaurs.]   I. Title. II. Series.
QE862.S3L38   1999
567.912—dc21   98-8279
                                                                    CIP
                                                                    AC

Contents

A group of *Velociraptor*

Speedy Thief

Picture a ferocious meat-eating dinosaur. Did you imagine a huge beast towering 20 feet (6 m) above you? That might describe some of the very large flesh-eating predators.

But there were also some much smaller dinosaurs that could be quite deadly. What

Velociraptor was small but fierce.

these dinosaurs lacked in size they made up for in other ways. Some were extremely fast on their feet. They may have been able to outrun their prey easily. Many also had long, sharp claws and strong, muscular bodies. Among these dinosaurs was one called *Velociraptor*. Its name means "speedy thief."

What were dinosaurs? Dinosaurs were ancient reptiles that lived on land. Like all reptiles, dinosaurs had scaly or leathery skin, lungs, and young that hatched from eggs with shells.

Like all dinosaurs, *Velociraptor* lived during the

Mesozoic era. This time period lasted from about 245 million years ago to about 65 million years ago. It is often called the Age of the Dinosaurs.

Velociraptor existed from about 80 million years ago to 70 million years ago. That was toward the end of the Cretaceous period–the last part of the Mesozoic era.

Fossils

Paleontologists are scientists who study prehistoric life. They learn about dinosaurs like *Velociraptor* through fossils. Fossils are plant or animal remains—such as bones, teeth, or tissue—that have been buried in the Earth's crust for millions of years. Over time, these remains, as well as the soil they are buried in, turn to rock.

Paleontologists have been able to figure out what different dinosaurs looked like by putting fossilized bones back

We know about dinosaurs through their fossils.

A fossilized skeleton of a dinosaur very similar to *Velociraptor*

together again. It's sort of like putting together pieces from a puzzle!

Velociraptor fossils have been discovered in China and Mongolia. Some especially interesting fossils were found

This map shows the countries in which fossils of *Velociraptor* have been found.

in Mongolia in 1971. These included a nearly complete skeleton of a *Velociraptor* locked in combat with a plant-eating horned dinosaur known as *Protoceratops*.

The fossils show *Velociraptor* using its front limbs to tightly grasp its enemy's head. It had used its sickle-shaped claws to rip open *Protoceratops's* belly. However, *Protoceratops* had caved in *Velociraptor's* chest with its horny beak. Both dinosaurs died in the struggle. Even so, the find clearly shows just how fearsome a predator *Velociraptor* was.

Fossilized remains of *Velociraptor* locked in combat with *Protoceratops*

Small but Fierce

Do you find it hard to believe that some dinosaurs were only 6 feet (1.8 m) long? That's just a bit more than the height of an average human male. Yet *Velociraptor* and its relatives are proof that such dinosaurs existed.

Velociraptor belonged to a dinosaur family known as dromaeosaurids. *Velociraptor* was the only dromaeosaurid with a flat snout. Most dromaeosaurids tended to be small. For a long time, the largest was thought to be only between 10 and 11 feet

This is how big *Velociraptor* would look next to a full-grown man.

A model of *Utahraptor*

(3 and 3.4 m) long. Recently, however, *Utahraptor* was discovered. Found in Utah, its name means "Utah thief." This relative of *Velociraptor* measured about 19.5 feet (6 m) long.

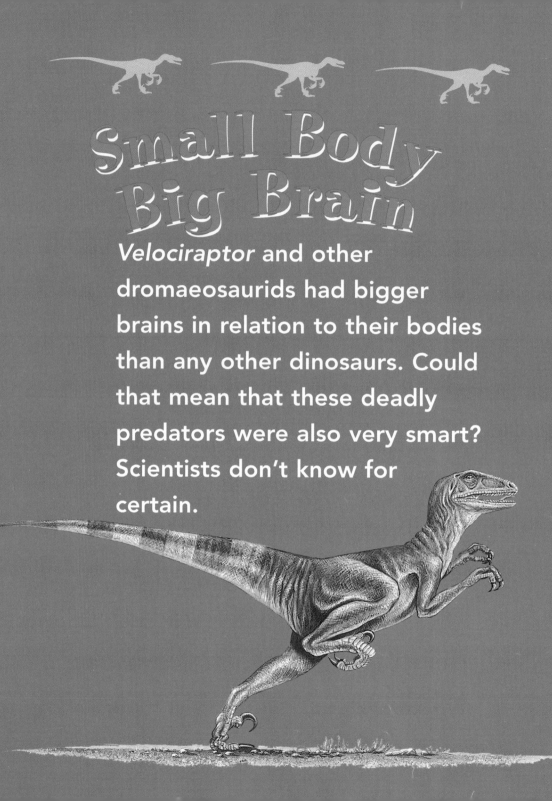

Small Body Big Brain

Velociraptor and other dromaeosaurids had bigger brains in relation to their bodies than any other dinosaurs. Could that mean that these deadly predators were also very smart? Scientists don't know for certain.

Velociraptor's 6-foot- (1.8-m-) long body was ideal for trapping prey. Its bones were so light that this dinosaur may have weighed no more than about 33 pounds (15 kg)! Its light weight and long legs helped make it among the speediest of dinosaurs.

Velociraptor had a long, narrow skull made of thin, light bones. This left enough room for the dinosaur's well-developed jaw muscles. These

were extremely powerful. One set of muscles allowed the dinosaur to open its jaws widely. Other muscles let its jaws snap shut tightly on its prey. A third muscle group made the *Velociraptor's* bite forceful enough to tear flesh easily.

Velociraptor's teeth were just as useful. They were long, sharply pointed, and jagged edged. Like those of other dromaeosaurids, *Velociraptor's*

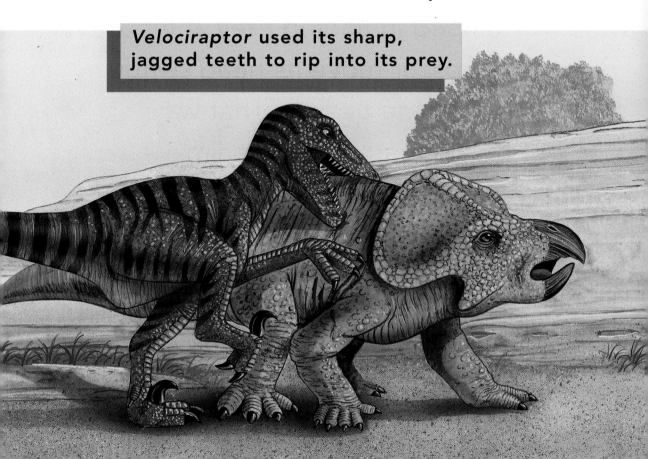

Velociraptor used its sharp, jagged teeth to rip into its prey.

teeth pointed backwards. By simply tugging, *Velociraptor* could quickly rip off a large chunk of its prey.

Velociraptor's slender neck helped in finding prey. It let the dinosaur move its head swiftly from side to side. That way, even a fast-moving animal would not escape its glance. *Velociraptor's* good vision was helpful in spotting prey as well.

This small dinosaur also had long, strong arms and hands.

Velociraptor claw

Each hand had three fingers with sharply pointed claws. *Velociraptor* probably used these claws to tighten its hold on its victims.

Like many meat-eating dinosaurs, *Velociraptor* held its

tail up stiffly when moving. But its stiff tail did more than just help the dinosaur keep its balance. By swinging its tail around, *Velociraptor* could change direction quickly. This was quite useful in chasing prey. *Velociraptor* never had to slow down, and often caught its victim easily.

Velociraptor is best known for its unusual feet. Each foot had four toes. Its first toe looked like a spur pointing backwards. Its second toe was actually a large, sharp claw shaped like a farmer's sickle. It was *Velociraptor's* best weapon for both killing prey and self defense.

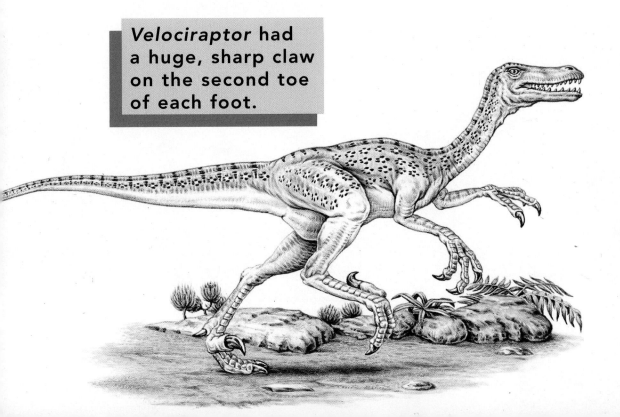

Velociraptor had a huge, sharp claw on the second toe of each foot.

Velociraptor attacking
Protoceratops

A Predator's Life

Velociraptor preyed on the plant-eating dinosaurs around it. At times it was able to bring down plant eaters much larger than itself. In these cases, *Velociraptor* may have used a type of prehistoric teamwork. Researchers think that *Velociraptor* sometimes hunted in packs.

Even then, it's unlikely that these predators attacked whole herds of huge plant eaters. Instead, they probably waited for a single dinosaur to wander off on its own.

A weak, young plant eater who had strayed from the herd would have made the best target.

Velociraptor probably hunted in packs.

A museum model of *Deinonychus*

First, several *Velociraptor* might strike at the plant eater's tail. Others would bite and tear at its hind legs. The final and most deadly blows probably came from a third group of *Velociraptor*. These would spring into action once the plant eater had stopped running. Using their sickle-shaped claws, they would tear open the victim's unprotected stomach and underside.

Velociraptor has often been compared to the dinosaur *Deinonychus*—another dromaeosaurid that was a small, swift hunter. It lived during the Cretaceous period

Museum models of *Deinonychus* are
sometimes shown with tigerlike stripes.

in what is now Montana and Wyoming. Like *Velociraptor*, *Deinonychus* hunted in packs and took on plant eaters much larger than itself.

In some life-sized museum models, *Deinonychus* has tigerlike stripes. This type of coloring would have been useful as it stalked larger animals. Blending in with the surrounding plant life, *Deinonychus* would not have been easily seen by its prey.

Of course, scientists don't know for certain what color *Deinonychus* was. They can't be sure of *Velociraptor's* coloring either.

The Dinosaur Disappearance

The Age of the Dinosaurs lasted about 150 million years. At different times throughout that period, various types of dinosaurs appeared and died out. However, no one type of dinosaur survived for that entire period. Instead, most dinosaur species existed for only a few million years.

Today, *Velociraptor* exists only in movies and in museum exhibits.

Paleontologists aren't sure why various dinosaurs became extinct when they did. They may have been replaced by other dinosaurs better able to handle the changing environment.

Fossils show that *Velociraptor* probably died out about 70 million years ago. Some of its relatives lived later on. But as of yet, there is no evidence that *Velociraptor* did.

Therefore, it's unlikely that *Velociraptor* would have been among the dinosaurs that died in what has come to be known as the mass extinction. This took place about 65 million

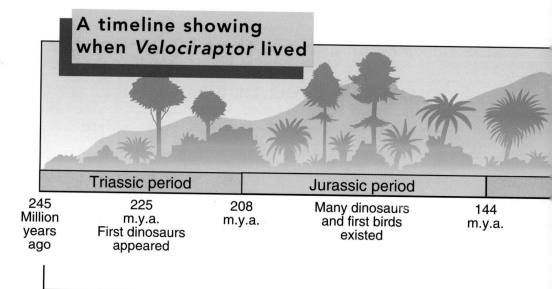

A timeline showing when *Velociraptor* lived

Triassic period		Jurassic period	
245 Million years ago	225 m.y.a. First dinosaurs appeared	208 m.y.a.	Many dinosaurs and first birds existed	144 m.y.a.

MESOZOIC ERA

years ago at the end of the Cretaceous period. At that point, all the dinosaurs left on Earth died out. Even this didn't happen on one day, but over a period of about a million years.

(Note: "m.y.a." means "million years ago")

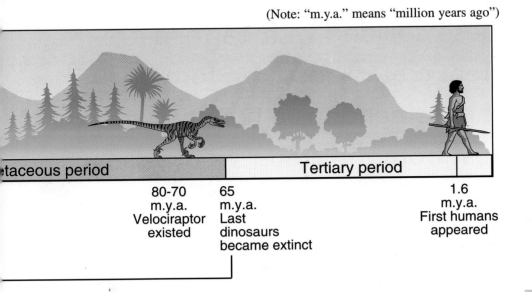

| taceous period | | Tertiary period | |

80-70
m.y.a.
Velociraptor
existed

65
m.y.a.
Last
dinosaurs
became extinct

1.6
m.y.a.
First humans
appeared

No one knows for certain exactly what took place.

One of the most popular theories among scientists is that an asteroid or comet about 3 miles (4.8 km) wide crashed into Earth. If one of these collided with Earth, a great crater would be formed. The tremendous amount of dust from the crater would rise up, forming thick, dense clouds. As these clouds blocked out the Sun, the

An asteroid may have been responsible for the final extinction of the dinosaurs.

weather would have turned cold. Dinosaurs and other forms of life would not have been able to survive this weather change.

Scientists are still debating the cause of the mass extinction. But they do know that the dinosaurs who died then will never return. Neither will those, like *Velociraptor*, who died out millions of years beforehand. We will only ever know this small, fierce predator through fossils.

To Find Out More

Here are some additional resources to help you learn more about *Velociraptor:*

 **Books**

Aliki. **Fossils Tell of Long Ago.** Crowell, 1990.

Cole, Joanna. **The Magic School Bus in the Time of the Dinosaurs.** Scholastic, 1994.

Henderson, Douglas. **Dinosaur Tree.** Bradbury Press, 1994.

Most, Bernard. **How Big Were the Dinosaurs?** Harcourt, Brace & Co., 1994.

Most, Bernard. **Where to Look for a Dinosaur.** Harcourt, Brace & Jovanovich, 1993.

Mullins, Patricia. **Dinosaur Encore.** Harper Collins, 1993.

Pringle, Laurence P. **Dinosaurs! Strange and Wonderful.** Boyd Mills Press, 1995.

Organizations and Online Sites

The American Museum of Natural History
Central Park West at
79th Street
New York, NY 10024
http://www.amnh.org

One of the world's largest natural-history museums, it has exceptional collections on dinosaurs and fossils.

DinoDon.com
http://www.DinoDon.com

Includes dinosaur art, a dinosaur dictionary, dinosaur news, and information on contests, digs, scientists, books, and links.

Dinorama
http://www. nationalgeographic.com/ dinorama/frame.html

A *National Geographic* site with information about dinosaurs and current methods of learning about them. Includes timelines, animations, and fun facts.

ZoomDinosaurs
http://www. ZoomDinosaurs.com/

Contains everything you might want to know about dinosaurs and other ancient reptiles. Its *Velociraptor* page includes facts, myths, activities, a geologic time chart, print-outs, and links.

45

Important Words

asteroid rocky object that orbits in space

comet frozen ball of water, gases, and
dust from the farthest reaches of our
solar system

continent one of the major land areas
of Earth

crater huge hole in the ground

detect to uncover or discover

devour to eat greedily

extinct something that has died out or
no longer exists

predator animal that preys on other
animals for food

prehistoric before humans began
recording history

sickle cutting tool with a short handle and
long, curved blade

Index

Meet the Author

Elaine Landau has a Bachelor of Arts degree in English and Journalism from New York University and a Master's degree in Library and Information Science from Pratt Institute. She has worked as a newspaper reporter, a children's book editor, and a youth-services librarian, but especially enjoys writing for young people.

Ms. Landau has written more than a hundred nonfiction books on various topics. She lives in Miami, Florida, with her husband, Norman, and son, Michael.

Photographs ©: AKG London: 18 (Johann Brandstetter); American Museum of Natural History: 11 (Beckett/Dept. of Library Services/2A21966), 20 (Finnin/Dept. of Library Services/2A21972); Animals Animals: 17 (Earth Scenes/ Eastcott/Momatiuk); Ben Klaffke: 2, 23, 26; Natural History Museum, London: 6, 25 (Orbis); Photo Researchers: 10, 14 (Francois Gohier), 4 (Chris Butler/SPL), 41 (NASA/SPL); Visuals Unlimited: 36 (A. Gurmankin), 30, 32 (Ken Lucas). Illustrations by Greg Harris